Out of the Shadows

Shine your light!
- woman of the womb ♡

Out of the Shadows:

The Shadow Work Workbook

Extended edition

Woman of the Womb

© 2021 by Ajané Searcy Rahman
Woman Of The Womb

Out of the Shadows: The Shadow Work Workbook
Extended Edition

Self-Published
womanofthewomb@gmail.com
www.themeditationfamily.com

ISBN: 9798504366166

This book is dedicated to the self healers who wish to make lasting changes in their lives and reconnect with their authentic selves.

- Woman of the Womb

TABLE OF CONTENTS

What you'll need to get started

An open heart

A journal dedicated specifically for shadow work and inner reflection

A few minutes to yourself as you work on these questions

Commitment to answering at least one question each day

Compassion as you come face to face with your inner self

1

What is the Shadow Self?

The 'Shadow Self' refers to the side of us that lies hidden within our subconscious. It is all things that lie dormant or suppressed within our minds, bodies, and spirits–both 'positive' and 'negative.' The Shadow Self represents our deepest fears and insecurities, things about ourselves that make us feel frustrated or ashamed, as well as our unrealized potential that is activated once can overcome these fears and insecurities. The challenges and weaknesses we have but don't wish to admit, are one aspect of the Shadow Self, but so are our innate gifts and talents that we hide from the world out of fear of criticism or rejection.

In short, the Shadow Self is where we hold onto all of our emotional baggage, which then becomes a catalyst for our emotional (rather than rational and logical) responses and things we project onto others. When we have not taken the time to address what is stored within the Shadows, we reject accountability for the power we have over our lives and often place the blame on others for why we feel the way we feel or why we react to things in the ways that we do. What many may not realize, is that by doing this, we hand our power over to those people to influence and control our inner state at any given moment. We become easily led and controlled by our emotions and triggers, rather than remaining in control of our vessel and our personal experience.

The things we suppress in the Shadows can manifest in unhealthy ways, including, but not limited to limiting beliefs that keep us from achieving our goals, inner tension, anger, rage, psychological stress, being triggered by someone else's words and actions, destructive feelings, toxic body image, negative self-talk, irrational thoughts and fears, mental, emotional, or physical health issues and diseases, self-sabotaging habits, repeated relationship patterns and cycles, and an inability to connect intimately and authentically with others (or ourselves for that matter). The severity of these symptoms that have the potential to manifest depends on how much we suppress and the amount of time we go on suppressing it; the longer we go without processing and dealing with these inner struggles, the greater their impact will be. The longer we go suppressing our passions, gifts, and talents, the heavier the weight of feeling unfulfilled, purposeless, and stagnant becomes. Think about it like the Shadow Self's cry for attention. Much like a child, The Shadow Self will continue to lash out and throw these 'temper tantrums' until we tenderly and lovingly embrace all that lies within this hidden realm. The Shadow Self only wants to be embraced, accepted and loved rather than shamed, ridiculed, or rejected.

2

How is the Shadow Formed?

The basis of the Shadow Self usually originates from our childhood experiences and the things that shape our views and perceptions of ourselves, others, and the world around us. As children, we are trained and conditioned according to what is deemed acceptable (or unacceptable) by our parents, family, teachers, peers, community, and society as a whole. These mindsets are not always stated explicitly, but can sometimes be implied or perceived through observation. Of course, this conditioning in itself is not always a "bad" thing—after all, we must learn how to interact with others and function in society in a way that is healthy and appropriate. However, at the same time that we are learning how to 'fit in' with others, we sometimes end up suppressing our natural urges to gain approval, acceptance, and attention from those around us. When we experience rejection or disapproval, this sends cues to our mind that our actions (or thoughts, or feelings) are inherently bad or something to feel embarrassed about or ashamed of. As we go through life carrying these feelings and hiding certain aspects of ourselves, this can create blockages in other areas later in life, which can manifest in a plethora of ways.

Sometimes this suppression or disapproval is not done maliciously; in fact, some caretakers may be unaware that they are even doing this. For example, a child may really want to learn how to play the drums, but perhaps the family lives in an apartment building and the parents cannot afford to have them making so much noise, so they don't allow the child to pursue this passion. On its own, this may not be seen as something that could have such an adverse effect or long-lasting impact. But what if this became a repeated pattern? The parents don't want the child to make too much noise, so they always get in trouble for playing too loudly, or watching the TV too loudly, or walking too loudly across the floor. What if this is something that child is constantly scolded for? Over time, this could manifest as someone who becomes quiet and withdrawn; who's rigid and has no true sense of fun or enjoyment; who is afraid to take up space and be seen; who doesn't know what their passions are, let alone how to pursue them. The parents' actions may not have been done with the actual intent of harming the child, but how their actions are *internalized* by the child is what makes all the difference.

Of course, this hypothetical example is one of those "best-case scenarios." For many others, abuse (whether it's mental, emotional, physical, psychological, or spiritual) inflicted by caretakers can very much be intentional, and the wounds left by these types of traumatic experiences can cause even greater damage to our sense of self. Perhaps even worse, are those who experience these types of abuses unknowingly, or who are in denial about the abuse that was inflicted upon them. In this instance, the Shadow Self may become even more difficult to recognize and acknowledge because these types of people may fail to see that there is anything "wrong" with them or how they were treated, therefore they may not see any error in their behaviors, patterns, or ways of thinking. They don't recognize the aspects of their programming that may be a detriment to themselves or those around them. No matter which end of this spectrum one falls, as adults, it becomes our full responsibility to begin the work of unraveling how we internalized our experiences and certain messages we received as children, and how they affect our present reality. That way, we can move on and reclaim our power over our lives.

This workbook is designed to assist you in working through the experiences you may have had in your upbringing, by helping you to observe some of the ways you may have internalized these past experiences. The purpose of *The Shadow Work Workbook* is to help you get to the root of "why" you do the things you do and think the way you think. The questions and prompts herein are by no means a comprehensive list, but they are a great starting point to assist you on the lifelong journey of self-discovery and spiritual awakening.

3

What is Shadow Work?

Shadow Work refers to the process of becoming more self-aware–through practices such as meditation, breathwork, journaling, studying family history, therapy, etc.–in order to observe the unconscious reasonings behind our thoughts, behaviors, and patterns. Shadow Work reveals the 'why' behind the things we choose to do. It means looking at all of the ways we have internalized our life experiences so that we can clearly see how our ego and identity was formed; and furthermore, how they impact all of our relationships and interactions with others, but most importantly the relationship and interactions we have with ourselves. When we work to understand the root causes of our actions, we can figure out how to recondition ourselves in a way that allows our true spirit to shine through; for us to find the strengths in all of the things we deem about ourselves to be shameful, taboo, or weak. Shadow Work teaches us how to find the balance between the two worlds (lightness and darkness) so that we can constructively and creatively channel and direct the energy of the Shadow Self.

For example, someone who is sensitive and empathic may struggle with suppressed feelings of rejection and abandonment, and because of this, they may utilize their gifts (of sensitivity and empathy) in a way that causes them to suffer from codependency or over-giving and keeps them trapped in negative relationships cycles (trapped in the Shadow Self experience). These same qualities–if given proper boundaries–would also make them a great nurturer or healer. Doing the work to understand the root triggers–the first experiences that ever caused them to feel rejected or abandoned–can help them to transmute these gifts and utilize them in a way that is more beneficial. It allows them to fully step into that role as a nurturer or a healer, yet now equipped with discernment and the ability to set proper boundaries so that they can do their work without fear of being taken advantage of. They have done the work to transmute their Shadow Self experience, and have turned their gifts into something useful.

When we engage in Shadow Work (which is not just a one-time thing, but an ongoing process of continuous self-reflection) we have the opportunity to release these outdated perceptions. As we become adults, we develop the capacity to see beyond the limited perspectives and thoughts of a child so that we can let go of how we internalized the words, actions, and thoughts of other people. When you go out into the world and become your own person, you are being provided with a blank slate and opportunity. As an adult, you no longer (for the most part) have those same restrictions. Unfortunately, most people carry their past with them into the present, allowing them to miss out on this new opportunity and blank slate that's being provided to them–which is why Shadow Work is so important. If we have not let go of the past in our minds, if we do not do the work of clearing the energy of the past from our bodies and our spirits, then we will continue to restrict ourselves to the same patterns that are usually a re-

sult of coping and defense mechanisms we devel-
oped in childhood.

4

How to use the Shadow Work Workbook

The questions and writing prompts in this workbook are designed to help you get to the root of your "why?" As you journey through each question, hopefully, you are able to make the connection between your present thoughts, actions, and behaviors, and the root of where they all started. Some questions, you may have to alter or adjust if they do not necessarily apply to your specific circumstance or experience (for example, if a question asks about your mother but you were raised by someone else, then answer the question based on what applies to you). There are over a hundred questions and prompts in this book and we are going to go deep. **If you ever feel a strong emotional response to any of the questions because it triggers memories of a hurtful experience, pause and write about your emotional response in that moment. Discuss where in your body you physically feel it and as much as you can about the trigger, instead of responding to the prompt itself.** I encourage you to go at your own pace, skip questions you may not be ready for, and come back to them when you are.

Set a designated time where you can journal and explore the answers to these questions on your own. That way, if you need to cry, yell, or release, you can do so in a safe and intimate space. It's best to answer these questions during a meditation session and in-corporate grounding and body healing exercises, such as mindful breathing, dance or yoga. As the Shadow Self is just as much physical as it is mental, our healing work must also incorporate these two aspects. Journaling is to clear up our mental space, while movement is to clear up our physical. You may experience some physical tension in the parts of your body that correspond with specific emotions. Engaging in mindful movement and meditation helps bring your awareness to the places in your body where these emotions have been stuck and help them to pass. Along with mindful breathing, these techniques can also help you to stay grounded when processing difficult emotions.

One of the best grounding exercises you can do is to lay with your back flat on the ground, arms beside you with your palms facing down to the floor (you can also place your hands together in the shape of a pyramid and place them over your womb). Take a deep breath in through the nose, filling your lungs all the way up, to the point your stomach is visibly full and expanding outward. Hold your breath here for 5 seconds. Then, exhale through the nose, allowing your lungs to empty completely and your stomach to contract. Visualize everything being washed and swept away as you exhale. Repeat this cycle as many times as you need to until you feel yourself grounded and safe back in this present moment. Do this exercise before and after your journaling sessions. You can even stop and do this in the middle of answering questions if things start to feel to heavy. Always do something that uplifts you or brings you joy after engaging in these questions (like watching a comedy or taking a hot bath)–something that reminds you that you are loved, worthy and appreciated.

Remember that there are no right or wrong answers to any of these questions. Whatever comes up for you is both valid and important. Instead of answering these questions in your head, actually *write* the answers down (this is why I suggest having a companion journal dedicated specifically to your Shadow Work). When taken at face value, some of these questions may seem quite easy or simple to answer–but allow yourself to go deeper. Sit with each question for as long as you need and allow your subconscious mind to take over and see what comes up. You may be surprised at what you find.

To challenge yourself even further, you may even want to use the technique of writing your responses with your non-dominant hand; so if you are right-handed, try writing with your left or if you are left-handed, try writing with your right. This technique is great for allowing your inner child to come out (notice how writing with your non-dominant hand even resembles the handwriting of a child) and for accessing, activating, and strengthening neural pathways in the brain that have been lying dormant. Every once in a while, look back through your journal at some of your previous entries. There are some things that may not seem relevant at the moment, but in hindsight, you can form new connections and receive even deeper revelations.

Overall, this practice is simply to get you to become an observer of your Self; to get you to observe the motives and intentions behind your beliefs, thoughts, and actions. As we work to become more self-aware, we come to the realization that we are completely in control of all of our thoughts and our actions, and therefore we can learn how to become more in control of our life experience and what we are able to manifest.

SECTION I: The Journey Through the Womb

To begin the journey of Shadow Work, we must go back to the beginning; not just the relationship we have with our parents. No. We must go back even further than that. Not just the time you spent in your own mother's womb; but even further. Not even at the moment that you were conceived, but back even further than that. These moments *are* important and significant, and we *will* cover them in a moment; but for now, let's dig a little bit deeper.

There are certain things that we carry in our Shadows that don't just come from us and our first-hand experience; things that have their roots and beginnings with the ancestor of an ancestor of an ancestor. Depending on how much trauma has been passed down through one's bloodline, the amount of Shadow Work one has to do before they can even begin to process their *own* life experience can be heavy and enormous. Many people tend to overlook this aspect of Shadow Work because we are not aware or have not been taught the full scope of how energy is passed down through generations, specifically from one Womb to another, all the way back to the beginning of time. Every aspect of our journey through the Womb leaves a profound impact on the life that is being born into the world.

When a woman is pregnant–with a female child specifically–by the time that female child reaches 16 weeks (barely 4 months) gestation, she already carries within her ovaries, every single egg she will ever have in her lifetime. This means that when a woman is pregnant with her daughter, she is also quite literally carrying the future generations of what will grow to be her grandchildren. Therefore, whatever takes place while that child is growing within her Womb, not only affects the child but also leaves an energetic imprint on the future generations to come. This is why for many, the Shadow Work journey can be so deeply layered–because work must be done not only to explore the traumas that belong to *them*, but also to explore the traumas they've inherited that haven't been healed, cleared, or transmuted by the previous generations.

Perhaps there are certain emotions or energies that you may struggle with–certain habits, fears, or insecurities that you may have–and you have no idea where they came from or how they first began, or why you can't seem to shake them. Perhaps you had a wonderful upbringing, free of abuses or traumatic experiences, but there are certain addictions or toxic behaviors that you struggle with that just don't seem to add up. These things can often be attributed to the realm of the unseen–generational secrets that have never been dealt with. When one is unaware of the history of their lineage, they are unable to see in what ways they are simply playing out an old karmic cycle. They are unable to see that certain things they would normally attribute to their personality, identity, or life circumstance are not just some random occurrence, but actual patterns that repeat themselves as they are passed down through DNA.

To gain a full comprehension of this phenomenon and to understand that this is not just some 'woo-woo' pseudo-spiritual stuff, we must first begin by examining the element of Water and understanding how it works. Water is intelligent; it's programmable, specifically through sound frequency and vibration, and it holds onto memory. It is the oldest living element in existence, out of which everything else came into being. Water is the physical proof of our intricate connection to all living things, which we can see proof of when we think about the water cycle and how water travels, circulates, and transforms into different states depending on the conditions that it's in. It exists in the oceans, in the air, in the plants, under the ground, in the foods we consume, in our breath, in our blood, and it's constantly cycling through every one of these things at every moment— holding onto the memory of every place it once visited and traveled through. Water is the essence of life and without it, life as we know it would not exist.

When we understand how the bonds of water operate, we begin to see how certain cycles can be passed down simply through this water memory, and why the journey through the Womb is so important. Furthermore, it shows how our individual journeys through Shadow Work contribute to the collective healing of Mother Earth, its inhabitants, and future generations. What we heal within ourselves creates a ripple effect as water cycles through us and everything else. When we take the time to clean up and reprogram our "waters", we can alter the memories that are transferred from us onto other beings, and especially onto our children.

Just like the Earth, our bodies are made up of over 60-70 percent water. Blood in itself is comprised of water, and when a child is developing inside of the Womb, its own body of water is suspended and incubating inside another body of water–the amniotic sac–that's then suspended inside yet *another* body of water–the mother's body itself. Knowing what we know about water, how it's programmable and can hold onto memory, we begin to see how it is that we come to take on the memories of these generations past. We must understand that when a child is fully immersed in the water and the blood of the mother, it not only is being programmed by these past memories but also by every vibration that travels through the mother in that present moment; thus adding a new layer on top of the old memories that have already been encoded.

Every thought that the mother experiences, every word that the mother speaks or that is spoken to her, every action, everything she eats, how she feels about the child itself, what the relationship is like with the other parent, how the other parent feels about the mother, the energy surrounding how, when, where and even why the child was conceived–all of these sounds, frequencies, and vibrations program the child (and the seeds they carry) with a certain energetic imprint. When that child is born, they may not consciously remember any of this. But their bodies (that are also made up of water), hold onto the memory. All of that is what makes up the first and very deepest layer of the subconscious Shadow realm.

Of course, this not only applies to negative or traumatic experiences that can be passed down. This is also where generational gifts, ancestral wisdom, inner knowings, and intuitive messages are passed down as well. Passions that you feel drawn to, gifts and creative ideas that come naturally to you, inspirations and divine insight that seem to come to you out of nowhere, things you "know" but don't know how you know—these can all be imprints and influences from generations past. When we become aware of this, we can begin to channel and integrate the *healed* energy of those ancestors as well, to help us open up to our gifts and purpose in this lifetime, and to upgrade and carry on those legacies.

This first round of questions and prompts will take you on a journey of tapping into those memories of your journey through the Womb and beyond, and the energetic imprints that were left behind. If you do not know the answers to some of these questions, you may have to interview some of your family members to help you.

Journal Prompts

1. How did your parents first meet? How old were they?

2. How long were your parents together before you were conceived?

3. How old were your parents when they conceived you? What was their relationship like at this time?

4. How did your mother feel about being pregnant with you? How did your father feel about her being pregnant with you?

5. Where were you born? At home or in a hospital? Were you born early? Were there any complications? What are the details of your birth story?

6. Are you named after anyone in your family? If so, who? What do you know about this person? How do you feel about sharing the same name?

7. If you were not named after someone else, how did your parents choose your name?

8. What did your parents do for a living when they were pregnant with you?

9. Do you know your birth parents? If not, how does this make you feel?

10. Were you raised by your birth parents? If not, how does this make you feel?

11. What were your parents' relationships like with their own parents?

12. What are some stories about your family history that have been passed down to you?

13. What are some things that run in your family? This can be anything from health issues to personality traits. Which of these things would you like to avoid or let go of?

14. Draw out a family tree and see how far you can go back. What are some of the things you know about each of these people?

15. How would you describe your parents' level of self-esteem? Do you see any of these characteristics within yourself?

16. What roles do the men and women traditionally play in your family? What do you think about

these roles? Do any of them bother you? Do you feel as though you have to keep up with fulfilling these types of roles?

17. Do you know anything about your family's culture or ethnic roots? What do you know about them? Do you carry out any of these traditions today?

18. What are some questions that you've always had about your family? What are some family dynamics that made you feel confused as a child? Have you ever gained answers or clarity about these things?

19. Did your family immigrate to another country? What was this experience like for them? What sort of impact did this have on the family?

20. Which of your grandparents or great-grandparents have you met? Do you have a relationship with any of them? Did any of them pass away before you were born? Are you distanced from any of them? If so, why?

21. Share some of your favorite things or memories about your grandparents. Share some of your least favorite things or memories.

22. Do you know what your grandparents did for a living? What about your great-grandparents?

23. Did any of your grandparents serve in any war? If so, which war(s) did they serve in? What was their role? How did this impact them?

24. What is your family's financial history?

25. What do you know about the upbringing of your grandparents? How might their upbringing have affected their beliefs as parents?

26. How did your grandparents' beliefs impact your parents? Which of these beliefs did your parents carry on? Which beliefs did they do away with? What cycles did your parents continue and which ones did they break?

27. What things do you know about your parents' childhood? Where did they grow up? Who did they grow up with? How many siblings did they have? Were they the oldest or the youngest? Where did they go to school? Write down everything you know about this time in their life.

28. What are some traumas that your parents experienced growing up? How do you feel this im-

pacted their relationship with you? Do you feel as though they projected any of these things onto you? If so, describe how?

29. What's a secret that you know about your parents that you never told them you knew? How does knowing this make you feel about them?

30. Are there any health problems, mental health problems, addictions, or other issues/diseases that run in your family? If so, what are they? What do you think may have contributed to this?

31. Have you ever felt "different" from the rest of your family members? If so, in what ways?

32. What is a cycle, pattern, or family curse that you feel you have had to break? In what ways have you gone about doing so?

33. Did your parents have any special talents? What about your grandparents?

34. Are there any particular gifts, skills, interests, hobbies, or passions that you inherited from your parents or grandparents (or beyond)? If so, what are they?

35. Pick at least three family members to interview. If possible, speak to the oldest living person in your family. Ask them questions about their life and experiences growing up, their childhood, what their parents were like, something you have always wanted to know, etc. Think about some of the thoughts and feelings they may have had during these times. See if you can pinpoint any patterns or characteristics that you may share and write about them.

SECTION II: Family is Your First Community

The first home you have is inside of your mother's womb. The relationship that exists with her is the first one you will ever experience and sets the undertones for every other relationship that will ever follow. From there, this wave continues to ripple out into your material, physical home, where your relationships expand to include the father or other caregiver(s), siblings, grandparents, extended family, and eventually your peers, school, neighborhood, community, and so on.

The roots of how we interact with the outside world around us all stem from the very foundations of the relationship we have with our parents and the styles of attachment we formed with them, which again, goes back to even before conception. Our parents (and the families we grew up in) are our first opportunity to experience what it means to be in a community with other people: what behaviors are acceptable or unacceptable, how we relate and con-tribute to the environment around us, what is ex-pected of us, what we can and should expect and ac-cept from others, how we should be treated and how we should treat other people, what we need to do to have our needs met, how we are seen and valued, how we assess and determine our sense of self-worth, how we are to advocate for ourselves, and so much more.

The first seven years of a child's life are the most crucial and important, as this is where the basic functions that they will carry with them throughout life are taught and programmed into them. What a child is taught during this time, whether directly or indirectly, sets the foundations of how they will go out into the world once they leave their parent's home. It also sets a precedence for how they learn to show up for themselves and parent themselves when the time comes for them to be independent. This is the phase of our lives that models for us what self-care and showing up for ourselves looks like. These first seven years of programming are essentially a manual and "how-to" guidebook for children to learn how to navigate and maneuver through the world.

This is where we begin to develop most of our ideas and perceptions about life, ourselves, and other people. Our ability to trust, be vulnerable, display intimacy, and develop a sense of surety about ourselves are all deeply impacted during this phase of a person's life. This is why the Shadow Work journey would be incomplete without acknowledging the Inner Child, as the Inner Child is the main part of you that gets buried and hidden within these Shadows. The Inner Child represents that state of innocence and purity, and the limitless potential of who we are and who we can become before we are inundated by the projections of the world around us.

To reconnect with the Inner Child and explore these parts of you that you may have disconnected with, we will go back and recall some of these earliest memories, starting with your family and working our way out to the collective society as a whole. We will become the observer of these memories, not just to relieve the experiences of the past, but to ask ourselves: "How did this affect me?" "How has this influenced my thoughts and behaviors?" "In what ways do I see its impact showing up in my present-day life?" "Is holding onto this belief or perception helping me or hurting me?" and "Is this a behavior or a mindset that I need to let go of?"

All of the other sections of this workbook will stem from the foundation of the relationships you had with your parents (whether they are present or not), your caretakers, and the environment and home(s) you may have grown up in. We will explore how your experiences with these people and in these spaces have come to shape and influence your mind, beliefs, and perceptions.

Whether we are discussing the relationship you have with yourself, the relationship patterns you have with other people, how you handle and process your emotions, how you manage your money, your core wounds or deepest insecurities, we will always come back to revisit these childhood experiences; as this is often where we will find the roots to many of our inner struggles.

Journal Prompts

1. Who were the people that raised you growing up? Who were the other family members that you grew up with in your home? Describe your relationship with them and the way you all interacted with each other. Describe each of their personalities and the roles each of you played in the family. For example, who was the nurturer? Who was the quietest or most withdrawn? Etc.

2. How would you describe your role or position in your family growing up? What were some of the rules and expectations that were set for you? How did they make you feel?

3. What type of responsibilities did you have in your household growing up? What did you like or dislike about these responsibilities?

4. What expectations did you have of your parents as a child? Do you feel they met these expectations? If not, what do you think kept them from doing so? Which, if any, of these expectations do you feel may have been unrealistic? How have your expectations of them changed over time?

5. Discuss a time where you felt let down or disappointed by your parents?

6. What were some of your parents' core values? Which of these, if any, do you still hold onto today? Are any of them different and how so?

7. What common things did you get in trouble for as a child? How did this make you feel?

8. What things were you praised for the most as a child?

9. How many siblings did you have? What sibling order were you (oldest, middle, youngest)? What was your relationship like with each of them? If you were an only child, describe what that was like growing up.

10. What five words would you use to describe your home and family environment as a child?

11. Talk about your parents. What were their names? What did they do for a living? What was your relationship like with each of them?

12. Who did you look up to the most growing up? What did you like about them the most? In what ways did they influence your life? What are some

of the most important lessons that you learned from them?

13. Which traits did you like the most about your parents?

14. What traits did you *dislike* the most about your parents?

15. Which of your parents' traits–both positive and negative–that you saw growing up do you see in yourself now? When did you start to become aware of them?

16. What are some of your fondest memories from childhood?

17. What are some of your least favorite memories about your childhood?

18. What school(s) did you attend growing up? Describe your experience. What type of student were you? How were your grades? How do you feel you performed in school? What were some of your favorite subjects? What did you enjoy the most about school? What did you dislike?

19. How did you feel in relation to your peers? In what ways did you feel different from them? What were some common interests you shared with your friends?

20. Did you ever feel affected by peer pressure? If so, in what ways?

21. Were you ever bullied or ridiculed as a child? What for? By whom? What impact did this have on you?

22. Were you involved in any extracurricular activities? What were they? Did you enjoy them? If not, then what kept you from participating?

23. Describe your transition into your teenage years. In what ways would you say your interests and your focus changed? How did these transitions affect you in your school and social life?

24. Would you say you had a healthy level of privacy growing up? Did you have too much privacy or were your parents strict and not give you enough privacy?

25. What type of entertainment did you enjoy the most growing up? TV shows, books, video games, music, etc. What types of genres did you like the most? In what ways would you say the content of

these genres influenced your thoughts or your actions?

26. Talk about the place where you grew up. What was the town/city like? What were the people there like? What do you remember about the home you grew up in? Or did you move around a lot? If so, how did that affect you?

27. If you no longer live at home, at what age did you move out? What were the circumstances surrounding your leaving? Did you go away to college? Were you kicked out? How did you feel being independent for the first time?

28. If you still live at home, talk about what you look forward to about being independent. What are some of your fears about being independent?

29. Did you have a religious upbringing? What were you taught about religion or spirituality? Do you still resonate with those beliefs? How have those beliefs shaped your perspective as an adult?

30. Describe your relationship with your extended family. Do you have a large family (aunts, uncles, cousins, etc.)? Are you close to any of them? What were the core values of your family as a whole?

31. Can you recall any instances of family conflicts or feuds growing up? If so, what were they? How were they handled in your family?

32. How did your family exchange information growing up? Was it more private and secretive?

Was their gossip in between the smaller family groups? How did you feel about this?

33. What are some traditions that are important to your family? Do you still continue with any of these traditions today? Would you say you do so out of loyalty or obligation, or because you truly enjoy them?

34. Which relationships in your life–friends or family–no longer serve you and how so? Why do you feel you continue to maintain these relationships? How would you feel if those relationships came to an end?

35. What relationships or friendships do you have (or have you had) that you feel had a negative influence on you? Have you ever been a negative influence in someone else's life?

SECTION III: Who Are You, Really?

Now that we have concluded that just about everything you think you know, in some way, shape, or form, is a direct result of conditioning from your foundational childhood experiences, it's time to ask: Who are you, really? I mean, who are *YOU, really*? How much of you is *actually* you, and how much of you is just an accumulation of who you *think* you are based on what other people have told you, which comes from their limited views and perceptions of the world? How often are you acting based on recycled information versus following the actual voice of your inner compass? Are you able to differentiate between when it's your conditioning talking to you and when it's *your* intuitive voice speaking? Were you even aware that there was a difference? And how can you begin to unravel the two?

If you can acknowledge that everything you think you 'know' comes from your programming, then it should also bring you some relief to know that anything you want to change about yourself or your reality, can be done simply through reprogramming your mind to process and view things in a different way. You are not bound to programs and experiences of your past, or to the karmic cycles of the generations that have come before you. You can do the work to reprogram the memory of your water body.

The questions in this section will take you through your passions, desires, motivations, how you view yourself, your life goals, your aspirations, what you think your purpose is, how you define and identify yourself, and all of the things that make up who you are. We will sort through your beliefs about yourself and how they are influenced, and sometimes even compromised, by the thoughts and opinions of other people. This section is here to guide you in developing a stronger sense of self and improving your ability to tap into and trust your inner voice so that you can align with your authentic path.

We will not only explore how well you can hear this intuitive voice, but also how confident you are in listening to it, carrying out its directions, and staying true to this voice in the face of others. For every time we succumb to our fears, insecurities, or the projections of other people, every time we choose to hide certain aspects of ourselves and deny who we are at our core by suppressing our ideas, opinions, and creative gifts, we continue adding on to this false identity until we are no longer recognizable by even our selves. We begin living a life that is inauthentic because we are not being honest with ourselves, and we then end up attracting inauthentic people and experiences into our lives that we *know* deep down are lacking in substance or don't truly align with our values.

Getting back to the core of who you are allows you to take off the mask that you present to other people. By being your authentic self, you allow both you and the other person the opportunity to decide whether or not this is a bond or a connection that either of you wants to make. Not only is it unfair to you for you to pretend to be something or someone that you are not, but it is also unfair to the other person as it robs them of their opportunity to make a choice. You could save both yourself and the other person so much time by acknowledging upfront that you may not align with each other's values; and in doing so, you leave space for both of you to call in someone (or something) else that is in better alignment with either of your needs, goals, desires, and interests. You do not have to force a connection that is based on an inauthentic foundation.

The reason why most people find this so difficult to do is because of the fear of rejection or abandonment, which, you guessed it, also has its roots in our childhood conditioning. As children, when we do not form secure attachment styles with our parents or the closest people to us in our lives, when we receive the message that we are only loved, seen, heard, or validated when we comply with the demands of others, or when our needs are only met once we meet a certain standard or requirement, then we go out into the world performing, just as we were taught to do in the past. We quickly learn that there is a certain level of danger that may come along with going against the status quo; whether that danger is in the form of punishment, abuse, criticism, rejection, or disapproval.

As children, the only people we have to rely on are the ones who are closest to us. We depend on them for food, clothing, shelter, connection, and intimacy, so we can not jeopardize the bonds and relationships that we have, otherwise, this could result in some of our core needs not being met. We do not yet have the freedom to control how or where we want to move; our friendships are formed out of whoever is available at that moment, perhaps based on the school our parents chose for us or the activities they allowed us to participate in. In a sense, we had to pick from the selection we were given, whether these connections truly aligned with us or not. We did what we had to do to survive and create some sort of sense of community. Even if that means suppressing certain aspects of ourselves to appease other people.

As we grow older, we hold onto these same subconscious beliefs that "these are the only people I have to choose from" and therefore, we cannot jeopardize the bonds and connections we have with them by speaking up and expressing our truth. We fail to realize that the world is a much bigger place than what we had access to when we were children;

that there *are* other people besides our families or childhood bonds that we have the choice and opportunity to align ourselves with. Our families may be our first community, but they are not our *only* community. We do not have to maintain bonds and connections with certain people simply because that is all that we know. We do not have to settle for just *any* type of connection, only for the sake of having *some* type of connection at all.

When we gracefully allow ourselves to be patient and say "no, thank you" to bonds and connections that do not truly align with us, we give ourselves the time and opportunity to say "yes" to the ones that do. However, to do this, we must first acknowledge and work through the subconscious fears of what we think will happen when we say "no" and begin implementing proper boundaries in our lives.

These boundaries are important because they set a guideline for the sacredness in which we treat ourselves. These boundaries allow us to develop a firm sense of who we are so that we know where our circle ends and where others begin and do not become confused or begin to blur these lines. Having this strong sense of self means you do not waiver or switch up every time you're in the presence of different people, just to be able to fit in. It is too exhausting trying to maintain this juggling act. It is much simpler, and much more fulfilling, to simply be ourselves and be "for" the people we are for.

Journal Prompts

1. What is the meaning of your name? Do you feel connected to this meaning? Did you like your name growing up? What about now?

2. Write a list of all the things that come to mind when you ask "Who am I?" Observe the words you used to describe yourself and see if there is a theme.

3. What was your favorite activity (or activities) as a child? How did this activity bring you joy?

4. Out of those activities you listed, did you stop doing any of them? Why? How did this make you feel? Did you ever get back to this activity?

5. What other things brought you joy as a child?

6. What were some of your talents as a child? Who was around you when you showcased these talents? Were they supportive or not? How did their responses make you feel?

7. What were some of the skills you had in school? What were your favorite subjects? Do you incorporate any of these things in your life today?

8. What is a skill you always wanted to have? What skills are you currently working to strengthen right now?

9. What would you say is your purpose in life?

10. What are your life goals? What do you believe are your main blockages in achieving these goals

(aside from money)? What are some things you can do to overcome these blockages?

11. What are some of your passions?

12. What creative things do you enjoy doing now as an adult? What are some of your hobbies?

13. What is something you enjoy doing that no one else knows?

14. How do you fill your time when you are bored? What forms of self-care do you practice regularly?

15. What skills, gifts, or talents do you have that you could use to help other people? In what ways could you help them?

16. What are things that bring you joy as an adult? Do you think you incorporate enough time for these things? If not, why?

17. Make a list of the things you love most about yourself.

18. What do you consider to be some of your weaknesses? In what ways could you see yourself using them as strengths? What do you consider to be some of your strengths? In what ways could they also be seen as a weakness? For example: if a weakness is that you are bossy, the strength would be that you are a good leader. If the strength is that you are determined and headstrong, the weakness might be difficulty accepting help from others.

19. What type of impression do you hope to leave on people when they first meet you?

20. What are some of the things you judge about yourself? Do you feel that other people judge you for these things? When was the first time you ever felt judged about something? What was it?

21. What values or opinions do you have that you feel uncomfortable sharing with your family or with others in general?

22. Whose opinions in your life do you value the most and why?

23. Do you feel as though you have to consult with others before making decisions in your life? Who else, besides you, has the most input when it

comes to decision making? How does this make you feel?

24. Have you ever felt guilty for making a decision in your life? Have you ever let someone down with a decision that you made? Who was it and how so?

25. What things do you feel are expected of you at this point in your life? Do you feel any pressure to live up to these expectations?

26. What are the expectations that you have for yourself at this point in your life? Why?

27. What things are you the hardest on yourself about? Why? And where do you think this stems from?

28. Do you ever feel as though you have to prove yourself? If so, in what ways?

29. Name a time where you went along with something that you knew was wrong or that you didn't want to do? Why did you choose to do it? What do you think would have happened if you disagreed?

30. What's one thing you know you need to do but keep avoiding? What is blocking you from completing this task? How can you overcome that blockage?

31. How would you describe your level of self-esteem? What experiences have contributed to or have hindered your self-esteem?

32. How does your self-esteem impact your decisions? In what ways do you feel your self-esteem helps or hinders you?

33. Finish this sentence: "In my ideal life I am..." Be as descriptive as possible. What things do you see? What sounds do you hear? Who is there with you? What does this life feel like?

34. What new habits are you working to cultivate? What old habits are you working to release? What (or who) is blocking you from forming or releasing these habits?

35. What are the best and most enjoyable aspects of your life right now? What things do you dislike about your life at the moment? What changes need to be made to alleviate some of those dis-

likes? How can you be more patient with yourself

as you make these changes?

SECTION IV: Emotional Intelligence

Emotional intelligence is a crucial skill that we must learn and strengthen as children to grow into mentally, emotionally, spiritually, and physically mature adults. This term describes our ability and capacity to recognize our own emotions, as well as the emotions of others, and how they all interact with and affect each other; to discern and properly label the emotions we are experiencing; to observe how we react and respond when we feel these emotional impulses and sensations within our bodies; to adjust and adapt our emotions in the face of changes and challenges; and finally, to utilize the information we receive from our emotions to guide our thoughts and our actions. How well we can complete each of these functions determines our level of emotional intelligence.

The basic skills necessary to maintain a high level of emotional intelligence are a result of both our innate characteristics (through our natural temperament as well as traits that are passed down through water memory) as well as our learned behaviors that come from the examples that are modeled for us throughout childhood. Our ability to navigate through life's complex emotions is heavily impacted by how our parents responded to our emotional needs as children, as well as the examples they displayed when handling their own emotional needs and responses. How we behave when we are angry, hurt, sad, confused, or overwhelmed; how we handle disagreements with others; how we respond to setbacks and failures; how we handle all the different challenges that life throws at us and manage our stress; these are all things that we learn growing up that are designed to assist us in navigating and interacting with the world around us.

Children naturally look to their parents and caregivers (or other authority figures) to provide clues on how they should regulate their own emotions, as well as respond to the emotional needs of other people. This is where our social cues and empathy skills begin to develop, but most importantly, where we learn to validate and regulate ourselves. Children who grow up in homes where they are allowed to express their emotions with proper boundaries and learn to regulate their emotions in healthy ways, tend to develop a higher level of emotional intelligence. They tend to have a more strengthened sense of self and an easier time navigating the ebbs and flows of their inner and external environments.

Children who grow up in abusive or traumatic environments, who felt 'invisible' or did not have proper outlets to express themselves, or who were denied the reality of their feelings and experiences, tend to struggle with their emotional intelligence and may often have a difficult time communicating their wants, needs, and emotions with other people in healthy ways. They may suppress their emotions or project their feelings onto other people since they do not know how to properly label the emotion they are feeling, let alone the source of where it's coming from. As they grow into adults who never learned the proper ways to deal with the emotion at hand, they lash out at the people around them. Instead of getting to the root of their emotional insecurities, they may take it out on their partner or their children and blame them for "making them feel" angry or insecure.

When a child learns to deny their emotions–like sadness or frustration–over time, will lose the ability to recognize when they are even experiencing these emotions at all. They eventually become so desensitized to the feeling of that emotion that they no longer recognize the moments when these emotions are occurring. However, just because they don't realize the emotion is occurring, doesn't mean that they aren't *acting* based on that emotion. And this is where the phenomenon of reacting versus responding to what's happening in the present moment comes from: it is our inability to connect with what is happening to us internally so that it can be expressed through the proper channels. A lack of emotional intelligence means that all critical thinking goes out of the window the moment this person's emotions are triggered. Emotions that started as a simple sadness or frustration, when left unaddressed, can become easily exacerbated and later manifest as issues with depression and rage, all while the underlying root causes go on being masked and undetected.

Just because a child learns to suppress an emotion, doesn't mean that the emotion simply goes away. That emotion (energy-in-motion) is *going* to find a way to express and release itself. Sometimes this will be done through a child acting out, other times it will be displayed through self-harm. As we get older, and the more of our emotions that we suppress within our bodies, these energies can begin attacking us from the inside out, manifesting as mental, emotional, psycho- and physiological, and even physical health issues, tensions, and dis-ease. They can begin to impact our relationships and connections with others, they can put us into a space of disconnect and self-isolation, and they can become a breeding ground for issues like anxiety, depression, and PTSD.

Those who develop a healthy level of emotional intelligence know how to observe their emotions, and then can take the proper steps to release these emotions from their body. Growing up in a safe and trustworthy environment provides them with an opportunity to talk about what they are experiencing, process it, hopefully, come to a resolution, and then move on. But for those who are not afforded this opportunity, the results can be severely detrimental.

The questions and prompts in this section are designed to help you assess your level of emotional intelligence, your coping mechanisms, how you relate to your feelings, and finally, how you communicate them with other people. We will explore the earliest memories that helped set the foundation for your ability to process and regulate your emotions, and the people who contributed the most to this part of your development. The questions in this section may also stir up any remnants of suppressed emotions that are stored within your body and in your subconscious mind. By finally giving a voice to these emotions and doing the work to release them, you create a clear pathway for your emotional energy to flow, you break through stagnancy and sickness in your life, and most importantly, you learn how to be present in the moment and stop responding to things based on the emotional triggers from your past. You finally get to the root of where your strong emotional responses are *actually* stemming from so that you aren't triggered by behaviors that remind you of events in the past that used to make you feel the same way.

Journal Prompts

1. What does it feel like to have your emotions belittled or downplayed? Think back to the earliest instance in your life when this happened and describe that time. Who was the person that made you feel this way?

2. What does it feel like to be completely discouraged by someone's words? Describe a time where you experienced this?

3. How would you describe your parents' communication style with you as a child?

4. How would you describe the way your parents communicated with each other? How did they handle conflict or disagreements with each other?

5. Write about the different ways in which people have expressed their anger or resentment in front of you. Would you say that any of these examples have affected the way you process and express these same emotions?

6. What was your parents' relationship like with each other? Were they together or separated? How did this affect you?

7. How did people in your household handle conflicts with each other?

8. Did you feel comfortable talking to your parents growing up? If not, who was someone you confided in the most? What made you feel safe confiding in them?

9. Are there people in your life now that you feel comfortable confiding in? Who? If not, what tools do you use to process or release your emotions?

10. Did your parents ever share any of their frustrations with you? If so, what were they? How did some of their frustrations make you feel about yourself?

11. What does the word "punishment" or "discipline" mean to you? How did your parents exercise discipline in the home? Did you agree or disagree with their forms of discipline? If you have children, do you see any similarities in how you discipline them now?

12. What healthy practices do you engage in consistently that help you to manage stress or other negative emotions?

13. Which emotion(s) do you tend to deal with in unhelpful or destructive ways? List some of these unhealthy habits. Who in your life may have displayed some of these same habits and coping mechanisms?

14. Observe the type of content that you consume the most frequently (tv shows, movies, music, people you follow online, etc.) and their most common themes and messages. How do you feel after you consume some of these things? How do you feel your life overall is impacted by these energies? Do you feel these energies ever affect your moods or your emotions?

15. In what ways do your moods or emotions affect your thoughts and decision-making?

16. How would you describe your outlook on life? Do you tend to approach things with more fear and skepticism? Or are you more optimistic and open to trying new things?

17. What are the things that bring you the most joy or make you feel the most at ease in your life?

18. How do you feel about change? How do you handle changes that occur in your life?

19. What emotion(s) do you try to avoid (sadness, jealousy, anger, weakness, etc.)? Why are you afraid of letting yourself feel that way? What do you feel it says about you to feel that way? Do you feel you are able to control yourself when you are experiencing that emotion?

20. What were some emotions that you weren't allowed to express growing up? What happened when you tried to express these emotions? How do these correlate with the emotions you tend to avoid now?

21. Are you open to other people's perspectives?

22. How do you handle constructive criticism? Do you ever feel triggered or offended by criticism?

23. How do you react when things do not go your way?

24. In what ways do you handle your setbacks and disappointments? Do you internalize them? Do setbacks make you feel negative about yourself? If so, explore why.

25. Do you ever find it difficult to admit when you are wrong? Why or why not?

26. Do you feel comfortable asking other people for help? Why or why not?

27. How do you show up for others but fall short in showing up for yourself? Explore why you have difficulties in creating a healthy balance.

28. Did you ever feel responsible for your parents' emotions? Discuss how this may have impacted your relationships as an adult.

29. How well are you able to keep commitments that you made to other people? How well do you keep the commitments that you make with yourself? If this is something you struggle with, what factors do you think may contribute to this?

30. Have you ever experienced someone using your emotions to manipulate or control you? Who was it? How did this make you feel?

31. Have you ever used *your* emotions to manipulate or control someone else? Have you ever used someone else's emotions as a way to manipulate or control them? If so, who was it? What was the result of this?

32. How do you approach conflict or difficult conversations with other people? Are you clear and upfront with them? Do you avoid and put these conversations off? What things do you fear about confrontation with other people? Why?

33. How well or how often do you prioritize your mental, emotional, spiritual, and physical health?

What are things you incorporate into your daily routine that support each of these areas? Do you think there are any changes you could make to give any of these areas more attention? How might these changes have a positive impact on your life?

34. Have you ever been heartbroken by someone? How did you react to this situation? Would you have responded differently? How did you overcome this time in your life? How did this affect you moving forward?

35. What about your life are you most grateful for?

SECTION V: How Do You Relate?

It is no secret that relationships–whether romantic or platonic–are a major challenge for most people. Which, should come as no surprise when we acknowledge the difficulties that most of us have with just being able to relate and be honest with ourselves. It often is not until we enter into a relationship with another person that we begin to see all these "ugly" parts of ourselves that exist in the Shadows finally begin rising to the surface. This is where we start to see the cracks in our communication styles, how we handle conflict, how we deal with our frustrations, and how we compromise with one another.

One of the main signs that someone is dealing with unhealed Inner Child and Shadow Work issues is when they begin to see the same repetitive cycles playing out in their relationships, or when they are constantly emotionally triggered. Rather than take a step back to ask themselves *why* these patterns keep occurring in their lives, or why they are so deeply triggered by their partner (or friends, or peers), most people end up shutting down, ghosting people, or jumping from one person to the next, expecting things to be different once they find the "right" one. Less often do they consider that the issues plaguing their relationships stem from what lies deep within their subconscious mind. Even worse, they end up projecting or blaming the other person for why things went wrong or did not work out.

Even when it comes to people in abusive relationships or who continuously find themselves with narcissistic partners–while their partner's behaviors certainly are **not** their fault and those partners will have to work through their *own* Shadow Work issues–it is important for the person to also look within themselves to figure out *why* they allow themselves to endure such type of treatment or *why* they are attracted to these types of people in the first place. Whether the reason is an inability to set proper boundaries, difficulty with discernment, a lack of self-esteem, or simply playing out generational cycles, the issues within these relationships all have their roots somewhere. And this is where Shadow Work comes in.

When we have not taken the time to address our internal issues, our Shadow Self can interfere with our relationships, especially when certain aspects of our Shadows are triggered by other people. At times, our Shadows can create illusions and cause us to see things in a way that is not always accurate. Projection, blaming the other person, and an inability to rectify challenges in a way that is logical rather than emotional, are all possibilities that can arise when we haven't done the work to pinpoint exactly where our fears or insecurities are stemming from.

When simple conflicts--that could easily be resolved with a simple solution--turn into disputes, blowups, or even physical violence, then we know that the conflict is not really about the issue at hand, but about something much deeper. Here is where acknowledging and exploring our emotional triggers comes in. On the surface, it may seem like a couple is arguing about one thing, but what's happening underneath all of that can be feelings of insecurity, inadequacy, lack of appreciation, not being heard, being excluded, feeling controlled, fear of abandonment, and a whole host of other things. Often what is happening is that the situation occurring in the present moment is triggering memories of events that happened in our past.

Remember, the body (water) holds memory, so certain experiences that we've had, that have been suppressed, unaddressed, or haven't been healed, can show up later during moments that closely resemble or even subtly remind us of these past experiences. To break that cycle and free ourselves from this type of self-inflicted emotional manipulation, we have to learn how to take a step back and observe ourselves when these triggers arise and get to the real root of the issue. We have to be willing to be vulnerable with ourselves (as well as the other person we are engaging with) and admit that the present situation is triggering us, and then go back to see where that feeling is stemming from. Engaging in Shadow Work allows us to strengthen our ability to decide to respond in a new way, to create a new cycle going forward.

Of course, our emotional triggers are only one piece of the puzzle when it comes to dealing with the challenges that arise in our relationships. Our actual beliefs and expectations of who we are supposed to be, what we are supposed to provide, and the expectations we have for our partners and what they should bring to the table, are also important things we need to look at. What are the things that contribute to our overall beliefs about relationships and how we approach them? Many people enter into relationships with foundations that are built upon searching for someone to mask their insecurities, fill personal voids, or in a sense, act as the parent(s) they never actually had, and most times, they are doing so unconsciously. All of which, of course, contribute to the eventual breakdown of the relationship. By engaging in Shadow Work, we can learn to work through these challenges when they arise, or better yet, do the work on ourselves *before* we even enter into these relationships altogether.

The questions and prompts in this section are curated to help you explore your mindset about friendships, love, relationships, vulnerability, and intimacy and the examples and experiences that contributed to these beliefs. Of course, the relationship that we had with our parents, and even the relationship that they had (or did not have) with each other, plays a substantial role in how we learn to relate to other people. However, we will also explore messages that we receive from society--and especially mainstream media--that contribute to our beliefs and expectations about our relationships because they are just as influential in shaping our mindsets and beliefs.

Journal Prompts

1. Who in your life was the most encouraging to you growing up? What people in your life were the most discouraging? How did either of these experiences shape how you view yourself?

2. What does love mean to you?

3. Have you ever been in love with someone? What were the results of this relationship? How has this impacted your views on love? How has your definition of love changed since then, if at all?

4. What does it feel like to have your emotions belittled or downplayed? Think back to the earliest instance in your life when this happened and describe that time.

5. How did your parents behave when they were sad? Frustrated? Angry? Stressed? How do you handle these emotions as an adult now? Do you see any similarities?

6. What does vulnerability mean to you? Write a list of qualities you feel others should have that make you comfortable with being vulnerable.

7. What are the things that make you feel seen and validated?

8. How do you like for people to express their love to you? Are you comfortable receiving love and affection from others?

9. How do you display love and affection to the people in your life? Are you comfortable with sharing this side of yourself with others?

10. In what ways did your parents display their love and affection with you growing up? Would you have preferred they showed it differently? How so? How is it the same or how is it different now?

11. How do you approach difficult conversations with other people in your life? Do you find it easy to speak up for yourself? Why or why not?

12. What does having good communication mean to you?

13. How would you describe your communication style? How would you say others describe your communication style?

14. In what ways would you change the way you communicate with others?

15. Do you find it easy to communicate with your friends, family, or partner(s) about how they make you feel? Why or why not?

16. Do you accept responsibility when the people in your life tell you how your actions make them feel?

17. What traits do you have that you feel other people take advantage of? What type of boundaries do you think might help you to avoid this?

18. How comfortable are you with enforcing boundaries in your life? Who are the people you find it the most difficult to enforce your boundaries with? Why do you think that is?

19. How satisfied are you with your social life? What are some changes you would like to make regarding this area?

20. Who do you feel the most support and encouragement from in your life today?

21. List up to 5 people who are the closest to you. What qualities do you like the most about them? What are some things that make them special? Which of their qualities do you dislike?

22. Do you still have people around you that do not encourage or support you? Who? How does their

lack of support make you feel? In what ways do you feel obligated to keep these people around?

23. Who in your life would you say demonstrated examples of a healthy relationship? What types of qualities did these relationships exhibit?

24. Who in your life would you say demonstrated examples of unhealthy relationships? What types of qualities did these relationships exhibit?

25. What were the most common themes in the relationships you saw growing up? For example, were there a lot of divorces in your family, or were most people married? Were there ever any extramarital affairs or children? How did these patterns that you saw influence your thoughts about relationships?

26. What type of qualities do you feel a good friend should have? Do you consider yourself to be a good friend? What qualities do you possess that make you a good friend?

27. What qualities or beliefs do you have that you feel may negatively impact your relationships and friendships?

28. What are some of the positive qualities that you bring into your romantic relationships?

29. What are some negative or toxic qualities that you bring into your romantic relationships? Where would you say you learned these from?

30. How do you define romance?

31. What frightens you the most about romantic or sexual relationships?

32. Have you ever been hurt by or have you ever hurt someone you were romantically involved with? What happened? Hows did you overcome this together, if at all?

33. Describe your ideal partnership. What qualities would you want your ideal partner(s) to have?

34. Is there anyone in your life that makes you feel drained after spending time with them? What about them makes you feel this way? Do you think you possess any similar traits?

35. Who in your life makes you feel energized after spending time with them?

SECTION VI: The Things You Hide

This is perhaps the most important section of the entire book. After all, it's the things we hide, both from ourselves and from others, that makes it possible for the Shadow Self to exist. What most people do not realize is just *how much* it is that they are hiding and suppressing. In fact, according to scientific research, almost 90 percent of our total brain function is made up of the subconscious and unintentional aspects of our minds. Ninety percent! This means that only 10 percent of who we are makes it up to the surface to be seen by others. No wonder we struggle so much with authenticity, trust, intimacy, vulnerability, and connection when we spend so much timing hiding or in denial.

The most difficult part about all of this though is that because these things exist in the Shadows of the subconscious, most of the time, we don't even realize when we operate from this place of denial; and this is how the Illusion begins. We truly *think* we *are* being honest with ourselves and others when deep down, we *know* we are not. In an attempt to convince others that what we are displaying to them is real, we end up playing the role so well that eventually, we may even convince ourselves; for the longer we go on living the lie, the more real that lie becomes even to us.

Take a moment to think about just how much we actually hide: goals, opinions, ambitions, desires, dreams, creative ideas, life goals, hobbies, personal interests, feelings, words, love, fears, insecurities, addictions, health issues, etc. Of course, these are some of the most obvious things, but what about some of the not-so-obvious ones: the times we don't speak up when a person wrongs us; when we don't stand up for someone else who's being ridiculed; when we don't correct someone when they say our name wrong; when we let things slide that bother us all for the sake of "keeping the peace." What about the things we hide in our relationships like our past, our debts, our spending habits, our problems, our inner struggles, our expectations, our sexual needs or even sexual orientation, our wants and needs, or our family history?

Think about all of the reasons why we hide those things: fear of being rejected, thinking we'll be misunderstood, guilt, shame, fear of judgment, being left out or labeled as "uncool," not fitting in, not wanting to hurt other people, religious reasons, not wanting to labeled or stereotyped, etc. There are so many different reasons why we hide from others, but at the root of all of these things is some type of fear; Fear of whatever the anticipated consequence would be, should we open up and share the truth.

The questions in this section are designed to help you face the truth about some of the things you may be hiding. This is an opportunity for you to dive into the questions that you may not even want to ask yourself, things you likely have never shared with anyone else in your life. While some of these questions may be triggering for you, the purpose of answering them is to finally bring them up to the surface for you to deal with and begin learning to accept. By first being honest with yourself, you can gain a better understanding of the parts you want to bring more light to and display to the world, and this can help you to be more honest with the people in your life. The purpose is to help you rediscover some of the best parts of yourself, reconnect with some of your goals and your passions, and realign with your path and your purpose. At the same time, these questions will also help you to acknowledge some of the fears and insecurities that you carry that may be affecting your present-day life and relationships, and most importantly your ability to show up as your authentic self.

Who are some people in your life that you need to be honest with? If you are in a space where you feel as though you cannot have these types of conversations out loud with other people, then at least being able to journal about them allows you to free up space inside of yourself and your subconscious mind.

Journal Prompts

1. Take a moment to reflect on a few things you feel most ashamed of and explore why. What do you think would happen if people knew these things about you?

2. What are some of your biggest fears in life? Explore why and discuss some of the root causes of these fears.

3. What is your definition of failure? Is it something you are afraid of? Are there things in your life you feel you have failed at?

4. Write about a time where you messed up and needed forgiveness. Did you ask to be forgiven? How did this situation play out?

5. How did your parents handle things when you messed up or made mistakes?

6. What are some family secrets that you've held onto? How has holding onto these secrets impacted you?

7. Who are the people in your life that you seek the most validation and approval from?

8. What is something in your life that you feel guilty about and why?

9. What things in your life have you held yourself back from out of fear? Where did these fears stem from?

10. What's one thing you would do in your life if you had absolutely no fear of doing it? What about this thing makes you afraid to try?

11. Talk about a time where you did something hurtful to someone in your life. What were your reasons for doing so? Was it intentional?

12. Has anyone in your life ever betrayed your trust? Who was it? How did this make you feel? Did they apologize? How did this affect your relationship with them going forward?

13. Have you ever betrayed someone else's trust? Were you honest with them about your actions? Have you ever apologized to them? How did this affect the relationship going forward?

14. Is there anyone in your life that you would like forgiveness from? If you could talk to them now, what would you say? Write them a letter in your journal to come clean and release these feelings.

15. If you could say one thing to the person who's hurt you the most right now, who would it be and what would you say? Write a letter directly to them in your journal. Be brutally honest about the things you would be too afraid to say to them in person.

16. Write about one person you've never forgiven? What happened and what did they do? How has holding on to this memory affected you? Do you think you could forgive them now? Even if you feel as though you can't, write them a letter of forgiveness in your journal. Express what it

would feel like to no longer hold on to these emotions in your body.

17. What is something you need to forgive yourself for? Why haven't you forgiven yourself yet and do you think you are able to do so now? Why or why not?

18. What emotions tend to bring out the worst in you? Why do you think that is?

19. Discuss a recent situation that made you feel triggered? At what point did you feel the trigger arise? What was said or done that made you feel triggered? What events led up to that moment? How did you handle it? In what ways could you have handled the situation better?

20. What are some habits in your life that you feel you are not in control of?

21. What is a promise to yourself that you have broken or continue to break? Why do you think that is?

22. Talk about a time where you ignored your intuition or your first instincts? What influences made you do this? What were the consequences of going against your intuition?

23. Where in your life do you currently feel isolated and how are you dealing with that emotion?

24. What's something in your life that you feel you need to heal from that you've been avoiding? Why have you been avoiding it? What do you think will happen when you finally face this?

25. What do you currently envy about someone else's life and why? Who is this person? How can you work towards gaining the things that they have that you feel envious of? What things in your life do you feel may be blocking you from aligning with those things yourself?

26. What are some traits that you see in others that you wish you had?

27. What memories bring you shame? Think about who you were then, what led to your behavior, and how you've changed since. Now write out the words "I did the best I could at the time and I forgive myself."

28. What would you consider to be some of your self-sabotaging habits? Where do you think these habits stem from?

29. What are some of the recurring problems or conflicts in your life? In what ways might you be contributing to these issues? How do you play a role in the things that are happening to you? What actions could you adjust to avoid these things?

30. What unhealthy attachments (things, people, places, habits, etc.) do you hold onto? What fears do you have about ending these connections? What would be some of the benefits of ending these connections?

31. What makes you afraid of being seen by others? Name a few instances in your life where you were

the center of attention and made a mistake or felt embarrassed. How might some of these experiences contribute to your fear of other people "seeing" you?

32. Talk about something you've lied about in your past. What was it? Who did you tell this lie to? What did you think you would gain by telling it? What did you think you would lose by telling the truth? What was the result of the situation?

33. What are some things that you hide from your partner? What reasons do you choose not to share these things with them?

34. What are some things about your relationship that make you unhappy? What are some things that could be done to change this? What things would you have to adjust within yourself to make

some changes? Are these adjustments you willing to make? Why or why not?

35. What are some of the exact phrases or excuses that you say in your head when you block yourself from pursuing a passion or starting something new? Write them down so you will know and be aware the next time you use one. Explore the root of where these sentiments came from. Ask yourself what would happen if you could no longer use that excuse.

SECTION VII: Let's Talk About Sex

Speaking of the things we hide: sex, and all of its subcategories is one topic that seems to rank exceptionally high on that list. So high that this topic needed an entire section dedicated all to itself. This is perhaps one of the most complex, taboo, and hidden subjects (which is why I'm going to go ahead and insert a **trigger warning** here before we go any further) that also happens to be so simplified, widespread, and pervasive all at the same time. No wonder the topic of sex is the source of so much conflict and tension. We can see it, but not talk about it. We know that everyone has it (or else *none* of us would be here), yet we pretend that it is something that does not exist. We want to ask our parents questions, but they refuse to talk about it with us. We receive so many conflicting messages about sex, we have no idea how to control and utilize this energy. We can have it, but we'd better not talk about it. The less we talk about it, the more we begin to believe that it's dirty or shameful. The more dirty and shameful we feel about sex, the more dirty and shameful we feel about ourselves. And down the rabbit hole, we continue.

Talk about illusions and delusions. Imagine what this type of manipulation and confusion about a subject that is so integral to our fundamental existence does to the mind and the psyche. There is a very intricate reason for why the topic of sex is set up to be this way, and it all comes back to the Shadow Self and our life force energy. The less aware and in control we are of such powerful energy, the more we start to see issues arising in other areas of our lives; the more our life force energy can be drained, manipulated, and used against us.

The areas of our brains that are responsible for regulating our sexual arousal and desires are the oldest, most primitive, and animalistic parts of our brains. It's regulated by the same part of the brain (and by the same Root Chakra at the base of the spine) that's responsible for our sense of grounding, safety, stability, survival, fight or flight response, attachment, and fulfillment of our basic needs. Sex is the essence of life and the basis of how every one of us came into existence. Therefore, we can take it out of the context of just being a physical act that we engage in, and we can say that sex is simply a conductor for the energy of creation itself. It is the fire, the spark, the flame of pure potential that gives way to life. If sex can take something as tiny as an egg and a sperm and turn it into an entire complex human being (a whole universe unto itself), then imagine what else we can wield this energy to create. It's no wonder that certain entities would want to profit off of the unhealthy and toxic relationships that many of us have with sex. All so that we can be distorted in our ability to fully utilize our creative potential.

From harmful messages in mainstream media to sexual trauma, to sexual suppression, to sexual discrimination, to not being in control of our sexual urges, to even the sexual connection and energy our parents had when they conceived us, many factors contribute to our sexual energy being buried within the realms of our subconscious. And if we know that sex energy is the entire foundation upon which our existence is built, then we can see how this type of suppression or inability to regulate and be in control of our sexual energy can ripple out and affect so many other parts of our lives; mainly our ability to connect with and tap into our creative potential and overall sense of self and purpose.

Imagine if your parents had hidden secrets and resentment towards each other, and then they came together and had sex and conceived you. This energy is the foundation upon which your life force energy was built. Now imagine if those same two people came together, but this time, based on the foundations of love, honesty, mutual respect, and with the intent of creating a new life together. Then *this* would be the foundation upon which your life force energy is built. Now imagine the difference in the energy of those two children.

Think about how someone is initiated into sex and the long-lasting imprint that it leaves. Think about how people may suppress or hide their sexuality and see in which other areas of their lives they can feel held back, uptight, blocked off, or are lacking in confidence. Think about someone who grew up constantly being shamed or even over-sexualized, and how this can result in them hiding from the world, putting on weight so other people don't look at them, neglecting to care for themselves so they can thwart away unwanted attention. Imagine the impact that constantly hiding and shrinking oneself has on other aspects of that person's life. This is why reconciling our relationship with our sexual energy is so vitally important.

Becoming more in tune with our sexual energy has nothing to do with another person, who we're attracted to, or whether or not we're having sex with someone. Being in tune with our sexual energy, at its core, is about being in tune with and in control of our creative life force energy. It's about overcoming the obstacles that prevent us from having whole-some, intimate, safe, vulnerable, and consensual in-teractions with others in our lives–regardless of whether these are sexual connections or not.

We need to know that sex is not something that is simply limited to our physicality, and when we learn how to tap into this energy and utilize it in all of its various ways, we can create and give birth to all sorts of visions, dreams, realities, and whatever else our minds can conceive; but we can do it with a clear, channeled intent rather than out of chaos and confusion. When this creative potential is trapped in the realms of our subconscious, then it is essentially like trying to create a painting with blindfolds on. You may get some paint on the canvas and you'll end up creating *something,* but I guarantee the final picture will look nothing like what you intended. This is what happens we don't have a grasp over this aspect of our lives; we can end up attracting things into our lives that aren't fully in alignment with what we want.

The questions and prompts in this section will take you on a journey to explore all of your various beliefs about sex and where they stem from: from how you were introduced to sex, the messages you received about it, how your parents approached "the talk" with you--if they even did so at all--societal and media influences, and just how you relate to this part of yourself overall.

Journal Prompts

1. Describe your very first memory of sex. When did you first learn about it? Where or from who?

2. When was the first time you ever felt aroused? Who or what sparked that feeling?

3. What are some things you remember about going through puberty? What were some insecurities you had at this time in your life?

4. Did your parents ever have "the talk" with you? What are some things you remember them telling you? How did they approach the conversation with you? How would you describe the nature of the conversation?

5. At what age did you realize that your parents were humans too, and do indeed have sex? Write about how you found out, your reaction to it, how you felt, etc. Did you ever speak with them about it?

6. Outside of your parents, where else did you seek more information about sex? Who or what contributed the most to your sex education?

7. What are some things you wish you'd been taught about sex when you were younger?

8. At what age did you have your first boyfriend or girlfriend? Did your parents know about this? Did they approve? Were there any rules set for you in regards to this?

9. Describe the first time you introduced your significant other to your immediate family. How did they respond? How did this make you feel?

10. What were some of the beliefs you had about sex growing up? What about now? How have these beliefs changed over time?

11. What attitudes and beliefs towards sex were conveyed to you by your parents? By religious influences? By societal influences or influences in the media? Did any of these messages ever contradict each other? Which of these attitudes and beliefs did you internalize from them?

12. What does the word "intimacy" mean to you? In what ways other than sex can you practice being intimate with someone?

13. Do you feel comfortable with self-pleasure and exploring what type of things feel good to your body?

14. Other than sex, what are some ways you experience pleasure in your life?

15. Talk about your first sexual experience. Who was it with? How did it happen? What did you feel before, during, and after that moment?

16. Did you ever talk to your parents about the first time you had sex? Did you tell them immediately or after a long time had passed? How did they react when you told them? If you never told them, what was your reason for withholding that from them?

17. Do you feel comfortable having conversations about sex? If you have a partner, do you feel comfortable sharing your sexual preferences or needs with them? Why or why not?

18. Do you ever feel any shame about your sexual preferences? Why are why not?

19. Are there sexual experiences from your past that you feel ashamed of? If so, explain why.

20. Have you ever judged or shamed someone else about their sexuality?

21. Make a list of your past (and present) sexual partners and write a few words to describe each of those relationships. Do you notice any patterns? If so, what are they?

22. Have you ever used your sexual energy in a way that was harmful to others? How so? Has anyone ever used their sexual energy in a way that was harmful to you? If so, who was it and how did this affect you?

23. What struggles have you had with your sexuality?

24. Describe your most memorable or romantic sexual experience? Who was it with? What were the things you enjoyed the most? What qualities did this person have that appealed to you the most?

25. Besides physical attraction, what qualities do you consider before being intimate or having sex with another person?

26. How have your relationship standards changed over the years?

27. What character and personality traits do you find the most attractive about another person?

28. What qualities (other than your physical appearances) do you find the most attractive about yourself?

29. Have you ever felt insecure about your body? Or about a partner seeing your naked body for the first time? Have you ever been body shamed? By who? In what way?

30. Which parts of your body are you most insecure about and why? Which parts of your body do you love the most and why? Do you ever compare your body to other people?

31. Do you think a person's self-image affects the decisions they make about their sexuality? How would you say it has affected you?

32. Write ten positive affirmations about yourself. Then, sit naked in front of the mirror while you say them out loud. How does this exercise make you feel? Are you uncomfortable seeing yourself like this? If so, why?

33. Would you say that you are in touch with your sexuality? Why or why not? How has this changed throughout the years?

34. Describe some of your sexual desires or fantasies. Do you ever feel intimidated by some of these fantasies? Is there anything blocking you from experiencing these fantasies?

35. Are there any changes you would like to make in your sexual behavior, attitude, or thoughts? And if so, what are they? If you have a partner, what are some changes you would like for them to make? How do you think these changes would impact your relationship?

SECTION VIII: Money Matters

To gain deeper insight into how the Shadow Self impacts our relationship with money, we first need to shift our entire perspective on what we think money is. In its basic sense, money is a tool. It is a method by which we use to exchange value for goods and services. If we take away everything else that we associate with money (such as education, college degrees, jobs, careers, etc.) and we just look at money for what it is, we can see that in its true form, money is simply a conductor for energy exchanges to take place.

For many years, we have learned to associate money with "hard work," long years of studying, education, debt, struggle, capitalism, and just about every other negative connotation that we can think of. We even throw around phrases like "money is the root of all evil" when this could not be further from the truth. It's what people *do* with the money they have that makes them evil or not, which has nothing to do with the money itself. That person was likely already evil, well before they even had money.

Another word for money is *currency*, which can also be broken down into the word *current* or *flow*– words that connect us back with the theme of water, which we discussed in Section I. And what is money a flow of? Energy and creativity. It's as simple as that, nothing more, nothing less. Everything else that we associate with money is what creates these energetic blockages and dams up the flow of currency in our lives. Our inability to connect with our creativity, gifts, and talents and then turn them into something tangible and of value is what blocks many of us from flowing with the wave.

Most of our difficulties in this area stem from our conditioning and how we learned to approach money–by going to college, getting a good job, securing benefits, etc. But how many of us were taught how to use our abilities to create freedom in our lives? Not just financial freedom, but the freedom of time, the freedom to live life on our terms, the freedom to spend more time with our families, and the freedom to focus on the things we love and bring us fulfillment.

Another issue for most people is that they do not see the value in themselves and what they have to offer, and this is where Shadow Work comes in. For those who are entrepreneurs, this section is curated specially for you. As you venture on this journey of becoming more self-reliant, you have to understand that this is an alchemical process of learning how to convert your creative energy into physical matter. This journey challenges you to redefine what you think of as "valuable." The simple things you do every day, the things you know and are good at, the things you love and are passionate about–all of these things hold value. The alchemical process of money manifestation is about learning to convert all those creative ideas in your head into something tangible that you can offer to others for an *equal energetic exchange*. The biggest blockage comes from not being conditioned to see yourself in this way. All of the subconscious fears, negative self-talk, trauma, anxiety, insecurity, etc. that exist within the Shadows are the things that block you from being able to see your greatness. They block you from seeing how much value you can bring to other people's lives by sharing who you are and what you know.

Shadow Work exposes your insecurities and *why* you may be afraid to share your ideas and gifts with others: fear that maybe what you have to offer is not valuable, fear of people criticizing your work, fear of it not being good enough, fear of competing with everyone else in your field who is doing the same thing, etc. All of these fears have their roots somewhere. Perhaps the memory of an adult telling you "you will never make money doing that" or ridiculing you for your creative ideas in the past are what block you off from even trying to go after your dreams now.

We also have to be honest with ourselves and admit when *our* underlying traits prevent us from getting ahead. Instead of saying that making money is hard, we should be asking ourselves: Am I someone who tends to procrastinate? Do I struggle with being able to follow through with my plans? Am I inconsistent with the effort that I put into my projects? Do I lack the patience to sit down and learn from someone who may be more knowledgeable and can help guide me? After each of those questions, we then need to ask ourselves "Why?" We must take a hard look at ourselves and be honest about when our actions are not lining up with what we say we want.

Beyond the struggles that most people have with making money, are the challenges they have with keeping it and properly managing it. It is not enough to have the ability to make a lot of money if you do not know what to do to keep that energy properly circulating. These issues can range from poor spending habits and compulsive shopping to having anxiety about looking at your accounts and avoiding money talk altogether. Shadow Work allows you to look at the influences that contribute to your financial literacy so that you can begin to rewire these limited beliefs and poor habits. You will examine the overall temperament your parents displayed when they dealt with, talked about, and approached their money matters to see how some of these habits may have rubbed off on you.

Now, this section is **not** about convincing you to quit your job and become an entrepreneur! But for those who feel trapped by their financial circumstance, this is about doing the work to let go of the victim mindset and examining where your limiting beliefs lie when it comes to amplifying the flow of currency in your life. Whether or not you have a job, it is still necessary to learn how to tap into this power of creation and generate multiple streams for yourself so that *just in case* anything ever happened, you always know how to tap into your creative energy to sustain yourself.

Journal Prompts

1. How would you describe your family's financial status growing up? How did you feel about your family's financial status?

2. What did your parents do for a living? How did their work-life influence your family life?

3. Did your parents ever discuss money matters with you growing up? In what ways? What important financial values do you remember them teaching you?

4. Do you ever remember your parents being stressed about money growing up?

5. How would you describe your relationship with money now?

6. What does being "financially stable" mean to you?

7. What are some fears or insecurities that you have surrounding making money?

8. Does financial stress impact any of the relationships you have in your life? If so, in what ways?

9. Where do you feel it physically in your body when stress arises about money and finances? How do financial worries affect your moods and emotions?

10. Do you associate your financial status with your feelings of self-worth? How so?

11. Do you consider yourself to have any poor habits when it comes to handling money? How

responsible are you with managing your money? Where do you think you learned some of these habits from?

12. What type of education did you receive about money and finances growing up?

13. What material possessions did your family spend the most on when you were younger? How has this impacted your spending habits and what you deem as "valuable"?

14. How do you feel when you spend money? Do you spend without thinking about it or does it bring you anxiety when you have to spend money? How would you like to feel about spending money?

15. Are you comfortable discussing financial matters with your partner? Why or why not?

16. If you were to receive $5000 right now, how would you invest this back into yourself (outside of bills or debts)? How would you use this money to invest in improving your knowledge or skillsets?

17. What did you want to be when you were younger? How did those desires change as you got older?

18. What passion or career option would you pursue even if money were not a factor?

19. At what age did you first begin working? What was your first job? Did you enjoy it?

20. How did you spend your first paycheck?

21. Do you budget or keep track of your expenses? How do you organize your monthly expenses? Is this a task that overwhelms you? Why or why not?

22. What was your favorite job that you've had? What was your least favorite? Discuss why for each of these.

23. What important skills have you learned from the different jobs that you've had?

24. What is your current job or profession? How did you fall into this line of work? Is this something you see yourself doing in the future?

25. Do you feel the work that you do now is in alignment with your goals, interest, or passions? Do you feel this line of work aligns with your morals and your values?

26. How could you use your skills to create a career or business for yourself? What skills from any of your previous jobs could you use to support you in becoming independent?

27. Look back at the creative interests and hobbies you listed back in Section III. Brainstorm a list of 10 ways each of these could become a career (or a creative side gig).

28. What are some creative ideas or projects that you have been procrastinating on completing? How long have you been sitting on these ideas?

29. What fears do you have about putting your creative ideas and projects out there for other people to see?

30. Follow 5 people on social media who are successful in your field of interest. Journal at least 5 observations about them. What skills do they have that allow them to be successful at what they do? What types of services or products do they offer? What systems do they use to convey their offerings? Imagine yourself in their position. What qualities or skills do you think you'd need to have to maintain that level of success? Which of these qualities would you say you already have? What are some you feel you would have to work on?

31. What is your desired level of income? What would this income be able to provide for you both emotionally and materially?

32. What are your financial goals for your life?

33. What does success mean to you? What accomplishments are you working towards that will help you reach this level of success? What do you feel is currently blocking you from attaining this?

34. What is your ideal work situation? (Even if you consider this desire to be unrealistic).

35. Do you feel as though you have a healthy work-life balance? If not, what are some things you could do to change this?

5

What comes next?

You may have made it to the end of this workbook, but that does not mean that your Shadow Work journey ends here. In fact, the journey is only just now beginning. It is one thing to become aware of what has been existing in your Shadows, but now comes the part of the journey where you will need to learn how to rewire and reintegrate these parts of yourself back into the forefront of who you are. You are now being called to take all of this information that you have uncovered about yourself and do the work to reprogram the pieces that are hindering you from achieving forward progression in any particular area of your life. Shadow Work helps you to figure out where the "leak" in your life is happening before you can begin doing the work to repair it. After all, it wouldn't make sense for a plumber to start working on your kitchen sink when the leak is happening in the bathroom. Shadow Work helps you get to the root so that you know exactly what you need to work on to heal.

It is not enough to simply be aware of what our conditioning and traumas are or how they affect us, we must finally heal these aspects of ourselves if we wish to make any sort of meaningful changes in our lives. By taking the time to heal and reconcile these parts of ourselves, we can release feelings of guilt and shame, we can open ourselves up to more peace and pleasure, we can align with people who are a better reflection of our authentic selves, we can let go of tension and stress, and most importantly, we get to truly be ourselves so that our gifts and our light can shine through.

The purpose of this work is to get back in tune with your inner compass and be led by *your* connection to the Divine Source, instead of looking outside of yourself for the answers or for other people to guide you. You came into this world fully equipped with everything you need to be creative, prosperous, abundant, happy, joyful, and fulfilled. It is only when we begin to take on the projections of the outside world, that we begin to lose this sense of security in who we are, which takes our focus away from being in alignment with all of those things.

Thank you for showing up for yourself and for beginning the journey of healing. The future generations thank you for your dedication to self-healing and self-awakening.

About the Author

Ajané, better known as Woman Of the Womb, is a mother, wife, creative, author, and speaker who specializes in Womb Wellness, Shadow Work, and Inner Child Healing. Over the last 4 years, through workshops, intuitive readings, natal chart interpretations, and one-on-one spiritual guidance sessions, she works to assist others in discovering and overcoming their blockages to reclaim power over their lives and tap back into their abundance. With a combined following of nearly 200k on social media, she and her husband work together to influence and inspire others on their spiritual healing journeys. To learn more about her work, find her on social media <u>@WomanOfTheWomb</u> on all platforms.

Made in the USA
Columbia, SC
04 June 2021